Thumbtacks, Earwax, Lipstick, Dipstick

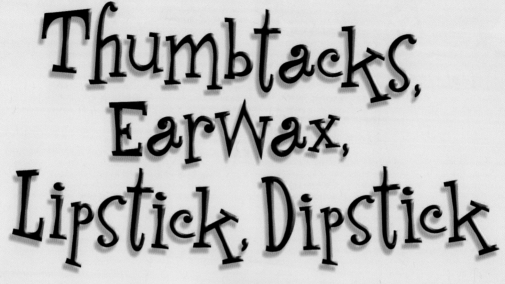

What Is a Compound Word?

To my mom, who taught
elementary school
before she had kids

—B.P.C.

Compound Word:
A word made up
of two or more
shorter words

Thumbtacks, Earwax, Lipstick, Dipstick

What Is a Compound Word?

by Brian P. Cleary

illustrations by Brian Gable

M MILLBROOK PRESS / MINNEAPOLIS

Compound Words

are single words

with other words inside,

like **sweatpants**,

cowboy,

horsemanship,

upstairs,

or worldwide.

5

Sometimes when we're reading,
we might see a big, long word,

then find it's made of smaller ones
as in this one: bluebird.

Same with armpit, undershirt,

outrun, and overgrow.

You'll cut those big words
down to size

When you see what they're made of:

Words you can pronounce and spell
and aren't a bit afraid of!

Words like **haircut**, dragonfly, cupcake, earring, freeway,

drumstick, lipstick,
chopstick, dipstick,

seasick, seafood, seaway.

earwax, thumbtacks, grandmother,

both longtime and longshoremen.

Compound Words

are mostly nouns—
that's people, things, and places—

like sunshine, ballpark, bulldogs, third baseman, and shoelaces.

Airport,

airplane,

runWay?

They're also compound nouns,

along with crosswalk, sidewalk, backyard, earthquake, and touchdowns.

These compound words
are adjectives,
and here are more for you:

the downtown mall,

the noonday sun,

a book that's overdue.

express some form of action,

like "connor liked to daydream when the class worked on subtraction."

Or "Molly used to jaywalk,
but now she understands."

And "Brendan outplayed everyone in both the marching bands."

When first you see these compound words, they may seem quite demanding.

But break them into smaller ones, and then you'll be outstanding!

So what is a compound word?
Do you know?

31

Find activities, games, and more at
www.brianpcleary.com

ABOUT THE AUTHOR & ILLUSTRATOR

BRIAN P. CLEARY is the author of the best-selling Words Are CATegorical® series as well as the Math Is CATegorical®, Food Is CATegorical™, Adventures in Memory™, and Sounds Like Reading® series. He has also written Six Sheep Sip Thick Shakes: And Other Tricky Tongue Twisters, The Punctuation Station, and several other books. Mr. Cleary lives in Cleveland, Ohio.

BRIAN GABLE is the illustrator of many Words Are CATegorical® books and the Math Is CATegorical® series. Mr. Gable also works as a political cartoonist for the Globe and Mail newspaper in Toronto, Canada.

Millbrook Press
A division of Lerner Publishing Group, Inc.
241 First Avenue North
Minneapolis, MN 55401 U.S.A.

Website address: www.lernerbooks.com

Main body text set in RandumTEMP 35/48.
Typeface provided by House Industries.

Library of Congress Cataloging-in-Publication Data

Cleary, Brian P., 1959—
    Thumbtacks, earwax, lipstick, dipstick : what is a compound word? / by Brian P. Cleary ; illustrated by
  Brian Gable.
      p.   cm. — (Words are CATegorical)
    ISBN: 978—0—7613—4917—4 (lib. bdg. : alk. paper)
      1. English language—Compound words—Juvenile literature. I. Gable, Brian, 1949-, ill. II. Title.
  PE1175.C55 2011
  428.1—dc22   2010051513

Manufactured in the United States of America
1 — DP — 7/15/11